LAST MINUTE REVISION

Standard Grade

CHEMISTRY
Booster

First published 2000
exclusively for WHSmith by

Hodder & Stoughton Educational
228 Euston Road
London NW1 3BH

A CIP record for this book is available from the British Library.

Text: Sheila Lynn, Gail Willey
Illustrations: Marcus Askwith
Developed and edited by Hart McLeod

ISBN 0340 78159 9

Printed and bound by Hobbs The Printer, Totton, Hants

An acid is a substance that releases **hydrogen ions** (H⁺) when dissolved in **water**.

Alkalis are soluble bases (metal oxides or hydroxides) which form **hydroxide ions (OH⁻)** when dissolved in **water**.

Air

Air is a mixture of 78% nitrogen, 21% oxygen and 1% noble gases, carbon dioxide and water vapour.

Oxygen and nitrogen are obtained by fractional distillation of air, since they have different boiling points (nitrogen b.pt. −196°C, oxygen b.pt. −183°C).

Test for oxygen – relights a glowing splint.

Test for carbon dioxide – turns limewater (calcium hydroxide solution) cloudy.

water vapour present in damp air (0–4%)

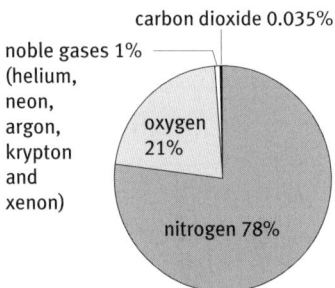

carbon dioxide 0.035%

noble gases 1% (helium, neon, argon, krypton and xenon)

oxygen 21%

nitrogen 78%

Pollutants may also be present in the air

See also **Nitrogen, Oxygen, Carbon dioxide**

Alkali metals

The elements in Group 1 of the Periodic Table are called **alkali metals**: lithium (Li), sodium (Na), potassium (K), rubidium (Rb) and caesium (Cs). They have similar reactions since they all have one electron in their outer shell (e.g. sodium (11e) 2.8.1) which they lose easily to form M⁺ ions.

Properties

- Extremely reactive, **stored** under **oil**, reactivity **increases** as you go **down** the group, Li → Na → K since the outer shell electron is lost more readily for larger metal atoms.

- **Shiny** when freshly cut, but **tarnish** quickly due to the formation of an oxide (reacts with oxygen in air), e.g.

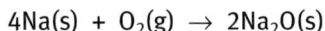

$$4Na(s) + O_2(g) \rightarrow 2Na_2O(s)$$

Continued overleaf

- React violently with water to form hydrogen gas and an alkaline solution of the metal hydroxide, e.g.

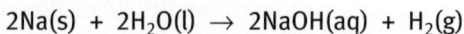

$$2Na(s) + 2H_2O(l) \rightarrow 2NaOH(aq) + H_2(g)$$

Alkalis *see Acids and alkalis*

Alkanes

A series of **hydrocarbon** compounds, each differing from the next by a $-CH_2-$ group i.e. **homologous series**. Carbon atoms are linked by a **single** covalent bond (C–C), i.e. **saturated hydrocarbons**. Each carbon atom forms **four** single bonds. General chemical formula is C_nH_{2n+2}

e.g.   methane n = 1   ethane n = 2   propane n = 3

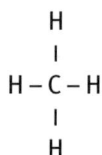

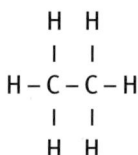

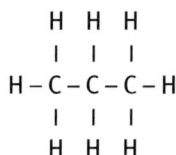

```
        H                    H   H                   H   H   H
        |                    |   |                   |   |   |
    H – C – H            H – C – C – H           H – C – C – C – H
        |                    |   |                   |   |   |
        H                    H   H                   H   H   H


      CH₄                   C₂H₆                      C₃H₈
```

CH_4 C_2H_6 C_3H_8

Sometimes it is possible to write more than one structural formula (**isomer**) for a single chemical formula, e.g. C_4H_{10} (chemical formula), structural formulae:

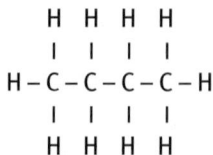

```
                                          H   H   H
                                          |   |   |
     H   H   H   H                     H – C – C – C – H
     |   |   |   |                         |   |   |
 H – C – C – C – C – H                     H   |   H
     |   |   |   |                           H – C – H
     H   H   H   H                               |
                                                 H
```

Butane   Methyl propane
(straight chain isomer)   (branched isomer)

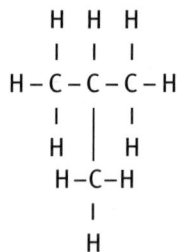

All alkanes from butane onwards have isomers. Alkanes are found in natural gas and crude oil.

Properties

- All have similar chemical reactions although they do not have many.
- **Combustion** is the most important chemical reaction, e.g.

$$\text{methane} + \text{oxygen} \rightarrow \text{carbon dioxide} + \text{water}$$
$$CH_4(g) + 2O_2(g) \rightarrow CO_2(g) + 2H_2O(l)$$

- Their major use is as fuels.
- Physical properties such as **boiling points** increase as chain length increases, e.g. pentane (C_5H_{12}) 36°C, hexane (C_6H_{14}) 68°C.

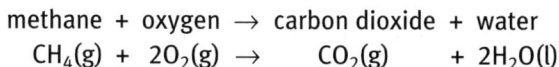
Alkenes

- Homologous series – general formula C_nH_{2n} (compare alkanes, see page 2).
- Contain one **double bond** between carbon atoms, i.e. **unsaturated**.

E.g. ethene C_2H_4 propene C_3H_6

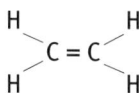 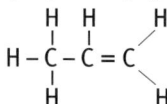

- They are more reactive than alkanes due to the double bond.
- They undergo **addition reactions** across the double bond, forming a saturated product, e.g. with bromine to form dibromoethane.

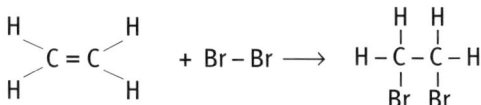

This reaction is used as a test for alkenes. The **brown/orange** bromine solution turns **colourless** when shaken with an alkene.

Alternative energy sources

Traditional sources of energy such as coal and oil will eventually run out. It is therefore necessary to look for **alternative energy sources**.

Continued overleaf

- **Solar power** – Energy derived from sunlight is converted into electricity using solar panels.
- **Wind power** – Windmills were previously used for grinding corn and pumping water; wind farms are now used across Europe to drive electricity generators.
- **Water power** –The force of tides can be used to generate electricity as the water flows through turbines (**tidal power**). Waterfalls and fast-flowing rivers also provide **hydroelectric power**.
- **Geothermal energy** – Rocks deep in the Earth are hot. Water can be pumped down onto the hot rocks where it is heated and pumped back up again.
- **Biomass** – Biological material is called biomass. Plants release energy when **burnt**, e.g. wood and coal. Plants produce **methane** when they **rot**. Methane can be converted to **methanol**, a liquid fuel.

Ammonia

Ammonia (**NH_3**) – very soluble, pungent alkaline gas (pH 11).

Industrial preparation – Haber process

Raw materials are **air** (to provide nitrogen – N_2) and **natural gas** (reaction of methane with steam at high temperature and pressure in the presence of a catalyst, to provide hydrogen – H_2). Summary of reaction:

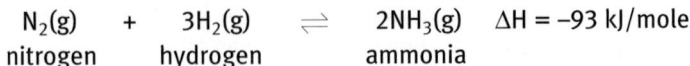

$$N_2(g) \quad + \quad 3H_2(g) \quad \rightleftharpoons \quad 2NH_3(g) \quad \Delta H = -93 \text{ kJ/mole}$$

nitrogen   hydrogen   ammonia

Exam tip
**Learn the conditions for a good yield of ammonia:
200 atm pressure, 450°C, catalyst of iron/iron oxides.**

Ammonia is used in the manufacture of fertilisers (see page 14), nitric acid, nylon, household cleaners, etc.

- All **atoms** consist of **protons** (+ve), **neutrons** (no charge) and **electrons** (–ve).
- The **nucleus** contains the protons and neutrons at the **centre** of the atom.
- Electrons **orbit** the nucleus in **shells**.

23	← mass number	12n
Na		11p
11	← atomic number	11e
	(2.8.1)	

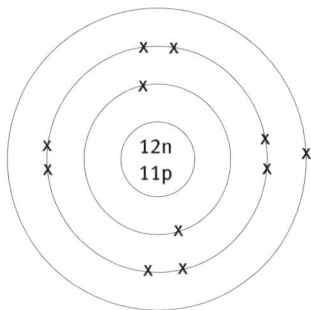

- Protons and neutrons have a **mass of 1**. The mass of an electron is negligible.
- **Atomic number (proton number)** – the number of protons in the nucleus.
- **Mass number** – the number of **protons plus** the number of **neutrons**.
- The number of **electrons** of an element **equals** the number of **protons** in atoms (so that they are neutral).

A base is a substance that reacts with an **acid** to form a **salt** and **water** only. The reaction is a **neutralisation reaction** in which the H^+ ions of the acid are converted to water, e.g.

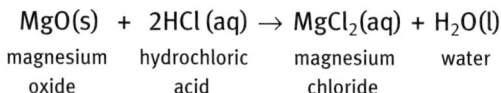

$$MgO(s) \ + \ 2HCl\,(aq) \rightarrow MgCl_2(aq) + H_2O(l)$$

magnesium oxide	hydrochloric acid	magnesium chloride	water

Examples of bases are metal oxides and metal hydroxides, e.g. copper oxide (CuO), calcium hydroxide ($Ca(OH)_2$), zinc oxide (ZnO). Alkalis are soluble bases (see page 1).

Carbon

Carbon occurs in two crystalline forms, **diamond** and **graphite**.

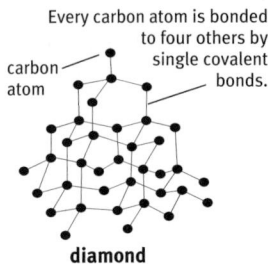

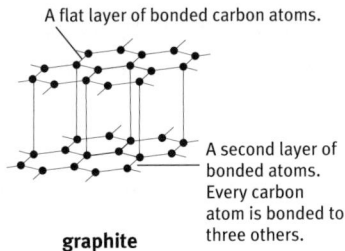

Every carbon atom is bonded to four others by single covalent bonds.

carbon atom

diamond

A flat layer of bonded carbon atoms.

A second layer of bonded atoms. Every carbon atom is bonded to three others.

graphite

The structures of diamond and graphite explain their properties.

Diamond	Graphite
Very hard – each atom is held in place by four strong covalent bonds forming a giant lattice. Used in industry for cutting, grinding and drilling. Attractive and rare and is therefore used for jewellery.	Soft and slippery – the layers of atoms slide over each other easily. Used as a lubricant and in pencil leads.
Does not conduct electricity – there are no free electrons to form an electric current; the electrons are held in covalent bonds and cannot move.	Conducts electricity – each atom has four outer electrons but forms only three bonds. The fourth electron moves through the structure and is free to conduct an electric current. Used for electrodes in electrolysis.
Very high melting point (3550°C) – the strong covalent bonds prevent each carbon atom from easily breaking away from its neighbour.	High melting point due to the covalent bonding between carbon atoms in the giant structure.

Carbon dioxide

Carbon dioxide is present in **air**. It is the **source** of **all carbon compounds** in **living things**. It **solidifies** when cooled to −78°C (**dry ice**) and is therefore used to keep food frozen.

Reactions

- Does not usually support **combustion**. Used in **fire extinguishers**.
- Slightly soluble in water forming the weak acid **carbonic acid**. Solubility is increased **under pressure**; this property is utilised by the soft drinks

industry to make **fizzy drinks**. CO_2 is bubbled into water under pressure; when the cap is removed from a bottle the pressure decreases and the CO_2 comes out of solution causing the 'fizz'.

- Produced when metal carbonates react with an acid, e.g.

$$CuCO_3(s) + H_2SO_4(l) \rightarrow CuSO_4(aq) + CO_2(g) + H_2O(l)$$

- Produced during the combustion of fossil fuels, e.g. coal (carbon)

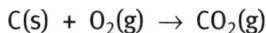

$$C(s) + O_2(g) \rightarrow CO_2(g)$$

Greenhouse effect is the result of the production of too much carbon dioxide which forms a blanket around the Earth preventing heat from escaping.

Test for carbon dioxide – turns limewater (calcium hydroxide solution) cloudy.

Combustion

Combustion is an **oxidation** reaction in which **heat** is **given out**. Combustion accompanied by a **flame** is **burning**. The combustion of **fuels** is one of the most important reactions. Fuels are needed to cook our food, heat our houses and run our cars, e.g. natural gas

$$\text{methane} + \text{oxygen} \rightarrow \text{carbon dioxide} + \text{water} + \text{energy}$$
$$CH_4(g) + 2O_2(g) \rightarrow CO_2(g) + 2H_2O(g) + \text{energy}$$

If there is insufficient oxygen present carbon monoxide(CO) is produced rather than CO_2. This is dangerous since CO is a deadly poisonous gas.

Compounds and mixtures

Compounds	Mixtures
A compound is a substance that contains two or more elements joined together by **chemical bonds**.	In a mixture the components are close together but they are **not chemically bonded** to each other.

Continued overleaf

A compound has a **fixed** composition. The elements are always present in the **same percentages by mass**, e.g. calcium carbonate as limestone, marble or chalk always has the composition by mass: calcium 40%: carbon 12%: oxygen 48%.	The components of a mixture can be present in **any proportions**.
A chemical reaction takes place when a compound is formed.	No chemical reaction occurs when elements form a mixture.
A compound has a completely **different** set of **properties** from its **elements**.	The properties of a mixture are the **same** as those of its **components**.
To split a compound into simpler substances a **chemical reaction** is required, e.g. water is electrolysed to hydrogen and oxygen.	**Physical methods** are used to **separate** the components of a mixture, e.g. a mixture of iron/sulphur can be separated by using a magnet to attract the iron filings.

Concentration of solutions

The concentration of a solution is the amount of solute, in grams or moles, that is dissolved in 1 dm^3 (litre) of solution.

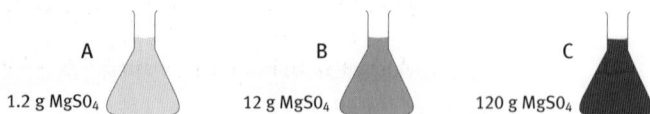

A
1.2 g MgSO$_4$

B
12 g MgSO$_4$

C
120 g MgSO$_4$

Flasks A, B and C, contain the same volume, 1 dm^3.
The mass of MgSO$_4$ dissolved in each is different.

Concentration in grams per dm^3.
A has 1.2 grams of MgSO$_4$ – concentration is 1.2 grams per dm^3
B has 12 grams of MgSO$_4$ – concentration is 12 grams per dm^3
C has 120 grams of MgSO$_4$ – concentration is 120 grams per dm^3

$$\text{Concentration in moles per dm}^3 = \frac{\text{amount of solute in moles}}{\text{volume of solution in dm}^3}$$

(See page 21 for definition of the mole.)

The formula mass of $MgSO_4$ is $24 + 32 + (4 \times 16) = 120$

A has 1.2 grams in 1 dm^3

$\quad$ 1.2 grams $= \dfrac{1.2}{120}$ moles $= 0.01$ mole, concentration $= 0.01$ mol/dm^3

B has 12 grams in 1 dm^3

$\quad$ 12 grams $= \dfrac{12}{120}$ moles $= 0.1$ mole, concentration $= 0.1$ mol/dm^3

C has 120 grams in 1 dm^3

$\quad$ 120 grams $= \dfrac{120}{120}$ moles $= 1.0$ mole, concentration $= 1.0$ mol/dm^3

Covalent bonding

Covalent bonding is the **sharing** of electron pairs by atoms of **non-metals** to obtain a **full outer electron shell**. The covalent bond is a strong bond. Atoms held together by covalent bonds form **molecules**, e.g. methane (CH_4) or giant structures (*see* **Carbon**).

Double bonds are formed when 2 atoms share 2 pairs of electrons, e.g. $O = O$

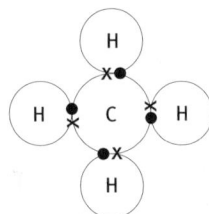

x = C electron $\quad$ ● = H electron
C in Group 4 (4e in outer shell)

Cracking hydrocarbons

The **breaking down** of large **hydrocarbon** molecules (compounds consisting of hydrogen and carbon only) into **smaller,** more useful alkanes and alkenes is called **cracking**. The process uses **heat** and a **catalyst.**

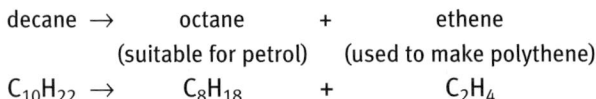

$\quad$ decane $\rightarrow$ $\quad$ octane $\quad$ + $\quad$ ethene
$\quad\quad\quad\quad\quad\quad$ (suitable for petrol) $\quad$ (used to make polythene)
$\quad$ $C_{10}H_{22} \rightarrow$ $\quad$ C_8H_{18} $\quad$ + $\quad$ C_2H_4

Distillation

This apparatus is used to separate a solvent from a solution – **distillation**. The solution is heated in the distillation flask; the solvent (steam) rises and passes through the condenser where it cools back to water and is collected in the receiver. The solute (salt) is left behind in the distillation flask.

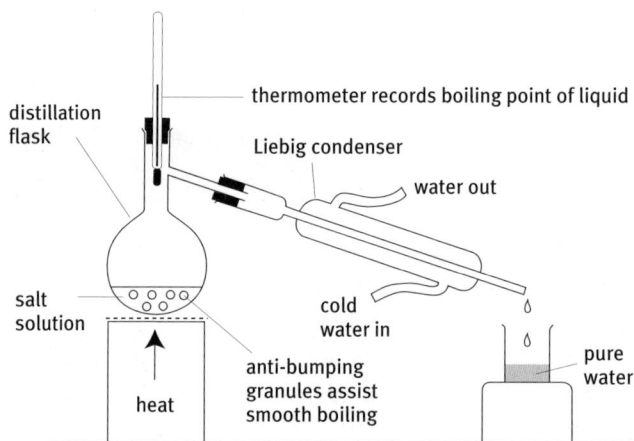

Apparatus for simple distillation

Electrolysis

The **break down** of a **substance** containing **ions** by **electricity** is called **electrolysis**. The **substance** that is broken down is the **electrolyte**. The process involves inserting two **electrodes** (conducting rods) into the electrolyte and passing a **direct current** through it. The electrode connected to the **positive** terminal is called the **anode**, and the electrode connected to the **negative** terminal is called the **cathode**. For electrolysis to be possible the electrolyte must be **molten** or **dissolved** in water, i.e. the **ions** must be **free** to move. Positive ions are attracted to the cathode and negative ions are attracted to the anode.

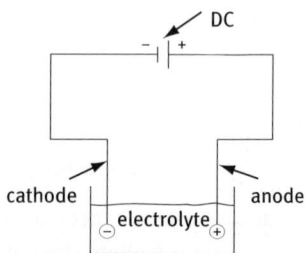

Apparatus used for electrolysis

Electrolysis – electroplating

Electroplating is the process of **coating a metal** with a thin, even layer of **another metal** using electrolysis.

- The object to be plated is used as the cathode.
- The metal required for the coating is used as the anode.
- A solution of a salt of the coating metal is used as the electrolyte.

Uses

- Steel is protected from rusting by electroplating with nickel and chromium.
- Tin is electroplated onto food cans to prevent corrosion of the can by food juices.
- Expensive metals, e.g. gold or silver, can be coated onto cheaper metals.

The object to be plated is made the negative electrode (the cathode).

The electrolyte is a solution of a salt of the metal.

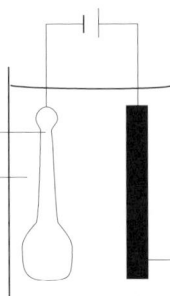

The positive electrode (the anode) is made of the plating metal. Metal atoms dissolve to form metal ions, keeping the concentration of metal ions in the solution constant.

Electrolysis – purification of copper

Electrolysis can be used to **purify** copper. This is how the process is carried out, to make pure copper for use as electrical wiring.

The cathode is a strip of pure copper. Copper is deposited on it as copper ions are discharged.

$$Cu^{2+}(aq) + 2e^- \rightarrow Cu(s)$$

The anode is a slab of impure copper. When a current flows, copper atoms go into solution as copper ions.

Cu ← Cu^{2+}

Cu^{2+} ← Cu

The electrolyte is copper (II) sulphate solution.

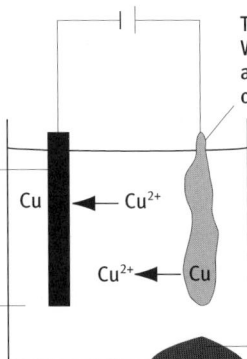

Anode sludge of impurities from copper anode.

Electrolytic purification of copper

Electrolysis – sodium chloride

The electrolysis of **sodium chloride solution** produces hydrogen at the cathode and chlorine at the anode. The electrodes used are **graphite**. Sodium ions and hydroxide ions accumulate in the solution. Gradually, the sodium chloride solution changes into a solution of sodium hydroxide.

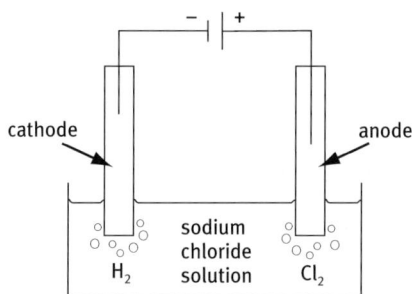

At the cathode
$$2H^+(aq) + 2e^- \rightarrow H_2(g)$$

At the anode
$$2Cl^-(aq) \rightarrow Cl_2(g) + 2e^-$$

Exam tip **Hydrogen is formed since hydrogen ions gain electrons more easily than sodium ions.**

Elements

Elements are pure substances that cannot be split into simpler substances. They are the building blocks of all matter. Every element has a **name** and a **symbol**, e.g. sodium Na, silver Ag, aluminium Al. Elements are classified as either **metals** or **non-metals**. Some of the physical differences between metals and non-metals are shown in the table.

Metals	Non-metals
Solid at room temperature (except mercury)	Gases, liquids or solids at room temperature
Shiny	Dull
Malleable and ductile – shape can be changed without breaking	Brittle (solids)
High melting and boiling points	Low melting and boiling points
Good conductors of heat and electricity	Poor conductors of heat and electricity
React with oxygen to form basic oxides	React with oxygen to form acidic oxides

Energy and chemical reactions

A **chemical reaction** occurs when chemical substances are changed into **new chemical** products. It may be **exothermic** – energy given out, or **endothermic** – energy taken in. Energy is absorbed to break existing chemical bonds; energy is released when new bonds are formed.

Equations

A chemical equation shows the **reactants** and **products** of a chemical reaction. An equation can be written in **three** different ways.

1 As a **word** equation, e.g.

magnesium + oxygen $\rightarrow$ magnesium oxide

2 As a **balanced symbol** equation – number of atoms of each element on the **left-hand** side must **equal** the number on the **right-hand** side, e.g.

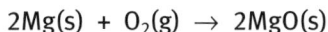

$2Mg(s) + O_2(g) \rightarrow 2MgO(s)$

3 As an **ionic** equation – only ions taking part in the reaction shown, e.g.

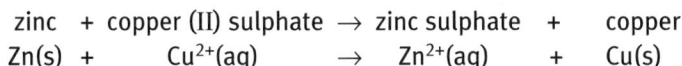

zinc + copper (II) sulphate $\rightarrow$ zinc sulphate + copper
$Zn(s)$ + $Cu^{2+}(aq)$ $\rightarrow$ $Zn^{2+}(aq)$ + $Cu(s)$

Exam tip ▶ **You must be able to write all types of equations.**

Ethanol

Ethanol (C_2H_5OH) is one of the homologous series of **alcohols**.

- It is a colourless liquid, miscible with water, and is commonly called alcohol – used in alcoholic drinks.
- **Burns** in air to produce **carbon dioxide, water** and **heat**; used as a fuel, e.g. gasohol, spirit burners.
- Slowly oxidised to **ethanoic acid** (vinegar) by air. This is why **wine** goes **sour** when left open to the air.

Ethanol can be manufactured in two ways.

1 **Fermentation** – yeast produces an enzyme (biological catalyst) that breaks down glucose from fruits, vegetables or cereals in the absence of air (anaerobic respiration). Used for wine, beer, etc.

Continued overleaf

enzymes in yeast
glucose $\rightarrow$ ethanol + carbon dioxide
$C_6H_{12}O_6(s) \rightarrow 2C_2H_5OH(l) + 2CO_2(g)$

2 **Ethene and steam** – passed over a strong acid catalyst (phosphoric acid) at a temperature of 300°C and a pressure of 65 atmospheres.

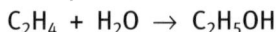

$C_2H_4 + H_2O \rightarrow C_2H_5OH$

Ethanol can be obtained from this mixture by **fractional distillation**. It is very pure – used as a solvent, fuel, etc.

Extraction of iron

Iron is extracted from **iron ore** (haematite) using a **blast furnace**. The raw materials required are **haematite (Fe_2O_3), limestone** and **coke**.

1 Hopper loads charge of iron oxide, limestone and coke into the furnace.

4 Carbon monoxide reduces iron oxides to iron.
$Fe_2O_3(s) + 3CO(g) \rightarrow 2Fe(s) + 3CO_2(g)$

3 Carbon dioxide rises up the furnace and reacts with coke to form carbon monoxide.
$CO_2(g) + C(s) \rightarrow 2CO(g)$

2 A blast of hot air enters. Coke burns in it to form carbon dioxide.
$C(s) + O_2(g) \rightarrow CO_2(g)$

8 Molten slag is run off (used for road building).

5 Hot waste gases leave – used to heat incoming air blast.

6 Limestone decomposes to form calcium oxide and carbon dioxide.
$CaCO_3(s) \rightarrow CaO(s) + CO_2(g)$

Calcium oxide combines with acidic impurities in the ore to form 'slag'.
$CaO(s) + SiO_2(s) \rightarrow CaSiO_3(l)$

7 Molten iron is run off (used to make steel).

Exam tip Learn the reactions carefully.

Fertilisers

Plants are a major source of **food** for the world's ever-increasing population. The **three** most important elements required for plant growth are **nitrogen, potassium** and **phosphorus. Fertilisers** are added to the soil to provide the plant with an adequate supply of these elements. These fertilisers must be soluble so they can be taken up by the roots. Fertilisers are chemicals such as **ammonium nitrate, ammonium sulphate, ammonium phosphate** and **potassium chloride**.

- **Ammonia** produced via the Haber process (see page 4) can be used to manufacture some of these chemicals.
- Ammonia is oxidised to **nitrogen oxides** ($NO(g)$, $NO_2(g)$) which in turn react with **oxygen** and **water** to produce **nitric acid**.
- **Nitric acid neutralises** ammonia or ammonia solution to produce ammonium nitrate.
- **Sulphuric acid** neutralises ammonia to produce ammonium sulphate.

Formulae of compounds

The formula of a compound is composed of the **symbol** of each **element** present together with the **number of atoms** of each of these elements.

For example, ammonia has the formula NH_3 which means it contains **1 nitrogen** atom and **3 hydrogen** atoms.

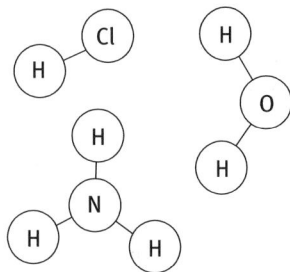

Fossil fuels

Fossil fuels are formed from **dead animals** and **plants** that lived millions of years ago. These were crushed under the pressure of earth and rocks and slowly decayed. **Coal, oil** and **natural gas** are fossil fuels.

Properties

- Release **heat** energy when **burned**.
- All contain **organic carbon** compounds.
- Produce **waste gases** when burned e.g. CO_2, SO_2, NO_x. Some of these **pollute** the atmosphere, and may harm plants and animals.
- They are **non-renewable** energy sources – the Earth's supply is limited.

Fractional distillation of crude oil

Crude oil is the main source of fuel in the UK. It is a mixture of many different carbon compounds (mostly hydrocarbons of various sizes). These can be separated by fractional distillation because each compound has a different boiling point. Each fraction is collected over its boiling point range.

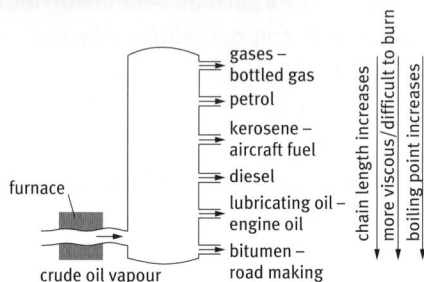

gases – bottled gas
petrol
kerosene – aircraft fuel
diesel
lubricating oil – engine oil
bitumen – road making

furnace

crude oil vapour

chain length increases
more viscous/difficult to burn
boiling point increases

Halogens

The elements in Group 7 of the Periodic Table are called **halogens**: fluorine (F), chlorine (Cl), bromine (Br), iodine (I) and astatine (At). They have similar properties because their atoms all have 7 electrons in their outer shell, e.g. Cl has 17 electrons arranged 2.8.7.

- They are extremely reactive **non-metals** which exist as molecules with 2 atoms (**diatomic**) e.g. Br – Br.
- They are all coloured (F_2 is a pale yellow gas, Cl_2 is a pale green gas, Br_2 is a red/orange liquid, I_2 is a shiny dark grey solid).
- They are poisonous.
- Boiling points/melting points increase going down the Group.
- Chlorine is used to purify water, make bleaches, disinfectants, antiseptics, pesticides and PVC plastic.
- Fluorine is used in toothpastes and drinking water as it reduces tooth decay. It is also used to make PTFE plastic for non-stick coatings.
- Silver halides when exposed to light, X-rays and radiation are converted to black silver, therefore used in photographic film.

Reactivity **decreases** going down the Group. **Reactions of halogens** involve the **gain of an electron** forming **halide ions**, e.g. $Cl_2 + 2e^- \rightarrow 2Cl^-$.

- Halogens react with metals to form salts, for example,

    sodium + chlorine $\rightarrow$ sodium chloride
    $2Na(s) + Cl_2(g) \rightarrow 2Na^+Cl^-(s)$

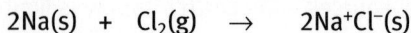

    Cl_2 is reduced to $2Cl^-$ ions; Na is oxidised to Na^+ ions.

Indicators and the pH scale

The strength of an acid or alkali can be measured using the pH scale.

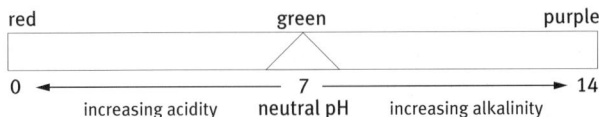

red — green — purple

0 ← increasing acidity — 7 neutral pH — increasing alkalinity → 14

- Acids have pH values less than 7.
- Alkalis have pH values greater than 7.
- pH 7 is neutral.

- The lower the pH the stronger the acid.
- The higher the pH the stronger the alkali.

Indicators are used to show whether a solution is acidic, alkaline or neutral.

Indicator	Colour		
	acid	alkali	neutral
litmus	red	blue	purple
methyl orange	red	yellow	orange
phenolphthalein	colourless	pink	colourless

Ionic bonding

Ionic bonding is one way of joining atoms together. It usually occurs between a **metal** and a **non-metal**. Electrons are transferred **from** the metal **to** the non-metal. The metal forms **positive ions** and the non-metal forms **negative ions**, e.g. sodium chloride (NaCl).

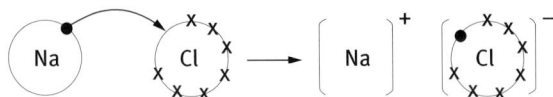

Sodium loses 1 electron
$$Na \rightarrow Na^+ + e^-$$

Chlorine gains 1 electron
$$Cl + e^- \rightarrow Cl^-$$

The **force of attraction** between the two ions of opposite charges is called an **ionic bond** (or sometimes an **electrovalent bond**).

The Na^+ ions and Cl^- ions bond together to form a **giant ionic structure (lattice)** as in the diagram.

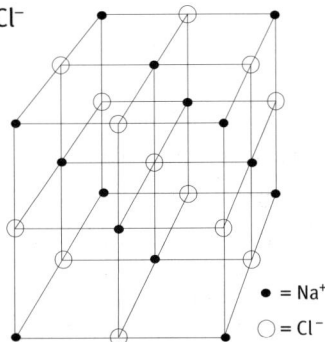

● = Na^+
○ = Cl^-

Exam tip   An ion is a charged atom or group of atoms.

Ionic compounds

Ionic compounds contain both **positive** and **negative** ions. The compound itself has no overall charge as the positive and negative ions balance each other exactly.

Examples

Magnesium chloride (MgCl$_2$) contains Mg^{2+} ions and Cl^- ions.
Two Cl^- ions are needed to balance one Mg^{2+}.

Iron(II) sulphate (Fe$_2$SO$_4$) contains Fe^{2+} ions and SO_4^{2-} ions.
One Fe^{2+} ion balances one SO_4^{2-} ion.

Metallic bonding

The outer shell electrons of a metal atom are free to move around. A lattice of closely-packed **positive ions** is surrounded by a **sea of electrons**.

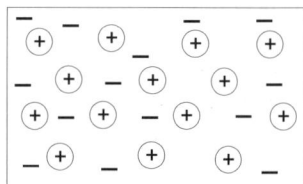

$(+)$ = sodium ion $-$ = delocalised electrons

The metal ions are held together by strong attractions (metallic bonds) to the electrons between them.

- They are good conductors of heat and electricity because the free electrons can move through the structure.
- They have high melting points and boiling points because a lot of energy is needed to break the metallic bonds.
- They are malleable (can be hammered into different shapes) and ductile (can be drawn into wires). This is because the layers of metal ions can slide over each other when a force is applied.

Metal ores

Most metals occur in the Earth's crust in rocks combined with other elements. Rocks containing **metal compounds** are called **ores**. Extracting metals from their ores is **expensive**. The rock is first mined, then crushed mechanically. A chemical method is then used to extract the metal.

The main ore of **aluminium** is **bauxite** (aluminium oxide, Al_2O_3). Aluminium is extracted by electrolysis. Purified bauxite (alumina) is dissolved in molten **cryolite** (another aluminium compound with a lower melting point).

At the cathode

$$Al^{3+}(l) + 3e^- \rightarrow Al(l)$$

Al^{3+} **reduced – gains electrons**

At the anode

$$2O^{2-}(l) \rightarrow O_2(g) + 4e^-$$

O^{2-} **oxidised – loses electrons**

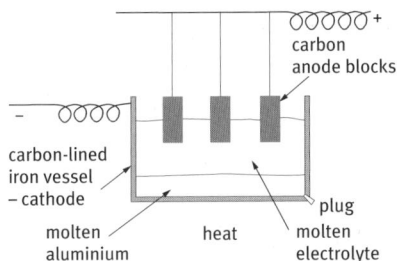

carbon anode blocks

carbon-lined iron vessel – cathode

molten aluminium   heat   plug   molten electrolyte

Iron is extracted from the ores **haematite** (Fe_2O_3) and **magnetite** (Fe_3O_4) in a blast furnace. (See page 14.)

Metals and alloys

The way a metal is used depends upon its properties. Some metals are useful in their **pure** state, e.g. **copper** in electrical wiring. Metals are often mixed with other elements to form **alloys** which are stronger and have better corrosion resistance. Alloys have different properties from the metals or non-metals of which they are composed.

metal/alloy	characteristics	uses
brass, an alloy of copper and zinc	golden colour, harder than copper, resists corrosion	ships' propellers, taps, screws, electrical fittings
bronze, an alloy of copper and tin	hard, sonorous, resistant to corrosion	coins, medals, statues, springs, church bells
copper	good electrical conductor, resists corrosion	electrical circuits, water pipes and tanks
iron	hard, strong, inexpensive, rusts	construction
lead	dense, unreactive, soft, not very strong	car batteries, divers' weights, roofing
steel, an iron alloy	strong	buildings, machinery, cars
tin	low in reactivity series	coating 'tin cans'

Metals and non-metals

Elements are classified as **metals** or **non-metals**. The differences in the **physical** properties are tabulated on page 12. The table below summarises the differences between the **chemical** properties of the metals and non-metals.

Metals	Non-metals
Able to donate electrons.	Able to accept electrons.
Form cations, e.g. Na^+, Mg^+, Al^{3+}.	Form anions, e.g. Cl^-, O^{2-}.
React with dilute acids to form salts.	Unreactive with acids.
The oxides and hydroxides are basic, e.g. Na_2O, CaO; when dissolved in water they form alkaline solutions.	The oxides and hydroxides are acidic, e.g. CO_2, SO_2; when dissolved in water they form acidic solutions.
Form ionic compounds with high melting points, e.g. $MgCl_2$, NaCl.	Form covalent compounds with low melting points, e.g. HCl(g).

Molecular solids

Some elements consist of **regularly** arranged molecules held together by **weak** intermolecular **forces**. Solid iodine is composed of I_2 molecules. The two iodine atoms are held together by a strong covalent bond.

- They have low melting and boiling points due to the fact that the molecules are held together by weak forces.

- Molecular solids are usually insoluble in water – unlike ionic solids.

- They are soluble in non-polar solvents and petrol – unlike ionic solids.

- They do not conduct electricity because there are no ions or mobile electrons present.

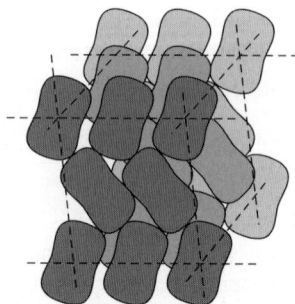

represents an iodine particle

One mole of an element is equal to its relative atomic mass in grams.
The **relative atomic mass** (A_r)(see page 31) of any element expressed in grams will contain the same number of atoms. This number of atoms is **6×10^{23}** and is called the **Avogadro number**. The symbol for mole is **mol**.

- 1 mol of **calcium atoms** has a mass of 40 g.
- 1 mol of **oxygen atoms** has a mass of 16 g.
- 1 mol of **oxygen molecules** (O_2) has a mass of 32 g.

The mass of one mole of a substance is called the **molar mass (M)**. The molar mass of calcium is 40 g/mol.

To find the number of moles in a given mass: $\dfrac{\text{number}}{\text{of moles}} = \dfrac{\text{mass}}{\text{molar mass}}$

Example

How many moles of magnesium are there in 48 g?

A_r of magnesium = 24

M of magnesium = 24 g/mol

$$\text{number of moles of magnesium} = \frac{\text{mass}}{\text{molar mass}}$$

$$= \frac{48 \text{ g}}{24 \text{ g/mol}}$$

$$= 2 \text{ mol}$$

To find the mass of a given number of moles:

$$\text{mass} = \text{mass of 1 mole} \times \text{number of moles}$$

Example

What is the mass of 2 moles of chlorine molecules?
A chlorine molecule contains 2 atoms: molecular mass is therefore 71.

$$\text{mass of 2 moles of chlorine} = 71 \times 2$$
$$= 142 \text{ grams}$$

Exam tip

Always make sure you know what type of particle is being referred to, i.e. number of moles of atoms or number of moles of molecules.

Neutralisation

Neutralisation is the reaction of **hydrogen ions** (from an acid) and **hydroxide ions** (from an alkali) or **oxide ions** (from an insoluble base) to give **water**. The ionic equation for the neutralisation process is:

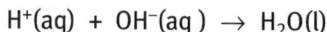

$$H^+(aq) + OH^-(aq) \rightarrow H_2O(l)$$

A salt is also formed as a result of this process. For example:

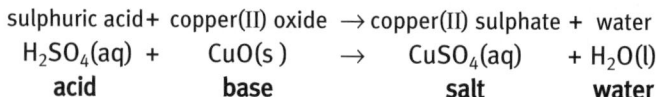

sulphuric acid + copper(II) oxide $\rightarrow$ copper(II) sulphate + water

$H_2SO_4(aq)$ +	$CuO(s)$	$\rightarrow$	$CuSO_4(aq)$	$+ H_2O(l)$
acid	**base**		**salt**	**water**

Applications of the neutralisation process

- In the production of **fertilisers** (see page 14). Solid fertilisers can be made by evaporating a neutralised solution.

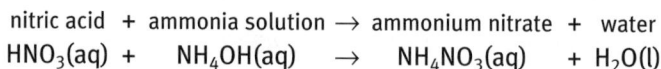

  nitric acid + ammonia solution $\rightarrow$ ammonium nitrate + water

  $$HNO_3(aq) + NH_4OH(aq) \rightarrow NH_4NO_3(aq) + H_2O(l)$$

- In the treatment of **insect stings**. Bee stings are acid and are neutralised by calamine lotion or baking soda. Wasp stings are alkaline and are neutralised with vinegar.

- Neutralisation of **acid soils** with lime (calcium hydroxide).

Nitrogen

Nitrogen is a colourless, odourless gas which makes up 78% by volume of air. It is obtained from liquid air by fractional distillation. The N_2 molecules have a strong triple covalent bond, which is difficult to break, making nitrogen a very unreactive gas.

Uses

- In the food industry for fast freezing and in the packaging of processed foods (replaces oxygen which would react with food).

- Liquid nitrogen is used when an unreactive refrigerant is required, e.g. to preserve organs for transplant and sperm for artificial insemination.

Nitrogen is the most important **plant nutrient**. It is required for the synthesis of **proteins**. It is used in the manufacture of **ammonia** (Haber process, see page 4) and **fertilisers** (see page 14).

Nitrogen cycle

The process in which **nitrogen** circulates between the **air,** the **soil** and **living things** is called the **nitrogen cycle.** The diagram below summarises the process.

Oxides of nitrogen (NO_x) form when nitrogen and oxygen combine in the air during a lightning storm, and also in vehicle engines and furnaces in factories. NO_x react with water to form nitric acid and reach the soil in acid rain.

The chemical industry makes ammonium salts and nitrates for use as fertilisers. These replace the nutrients which are taken from the soil when crops are harvested.

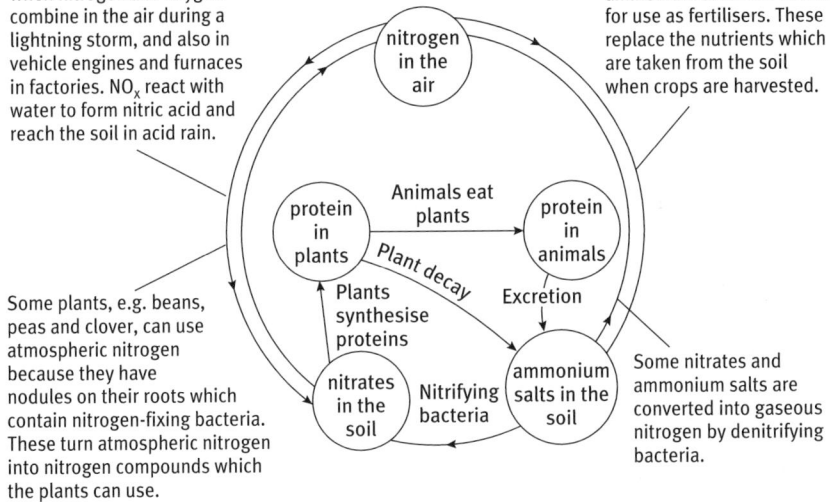

nitrogen in the air

protein in plants

Animals eat plants

protein in animals

Plant decay

Plants synthesise proteins

Excretion

nitrates in the soil

Nitrifying bacteria

ammonium salts in the soil

Some plants, e.g. beans, peas and clover, can use atmospheric nitrogen because they have nodules on their roots which contain nitrogen-fixing bacteria. These turn atmospheric nitrogen into nitrogen compounds which the plants can use.

Some nitrates and ammonium salts are converted into gaseous nitrogen by denitrifying bacteria.

Noble gases

The elements in Group 0 of the Periodic Table are called the **noble gases:** helium(He), neon(Ne), argon(Ar), krypton(Kr), xenon(Xe), radon(Rn). The properties of the noble gases are related to the fact that they all have **full outer electron shells**. They therefore have no tendency to **gain, lose** or **share** electrons and so are **stable unreactive elements**.
- All are colourless gases found in air in very small amounts.
- Very unreactive – exist as single atoms (monatomic).

Uses

- **Lighting** Argon is used in filament bulbs, neon in advertising signs and krypton and xenon in light-house lamps.
- **Inert atmosphere** Argon provides an inert atmosphere for welding and laser processes. This protects against any reaction with oxygen in the air.
- **Weather balloons** Helium has a very low density and is non-flammable so is used to fill balloons.

Oxidation and reduction

Oxidation is the **gain** of **oxygen**.
Reduction is the **loss** of **oxygen**.

Oxidation and reduction reactions occur together; these reactions are called **redox reactions**. For example, hydrogen turns black copper(II) oxide pink:

$$CuO(s) + H_2(g) \rightarrow Cu(s) + H_2O(g)$$

The copper oxide has lost oxygen and has been reduced, whilst the hydrogen has gained oxygen and has been oxidised.

An alternative definition in terms of electron transfer is:
Oxidation **I**s the **L**oss of electrons
Reduction **I**s the **G**ain of electrons   **OIL RIG**

Oxides

Oxygen reacts with many substances to form oxides. In general, metals react with oxygen to form **solid basic oxides**, i.e. will neutralise an acid to form a salt and water. The very reactive metals burn with bright flames, e.g. sodium, magnesium, calcium.

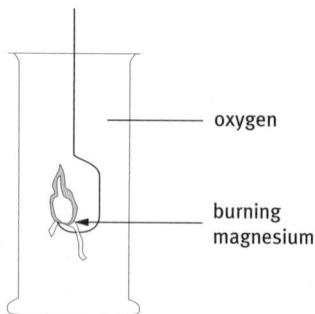

oxygen

burning magnesium

Ignited magnesium ribbon in a jar of oxygen burns with a brilliant white flame.
A white ash called magnesium oxide is left.

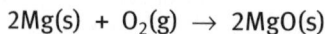

$$2Mg(s) + O_2(g) \rightarrow 2MgO(s)$$

Less reactive metals such as copper, iron and zinc react with oxygen when heated but do not burn. A layer of the oxide is usually formed on the metal. Non-metals usually react with oxygen to form **acidic oxides** which often dissolve in water to produce an acid. For example:

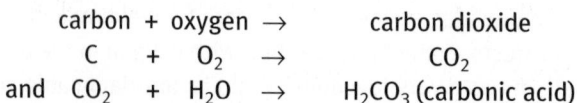

$$\text{carbon} + \text{oxygen} \rightarrow \text{carbon dioxide}$$
$$C + O_2 \rightarrow CO_2$$
$$\text{and} \quad CO_2 + H_2O \rightarrow H_2CO_3 \text{ (carbonic acid)}$$

Oxygen makes up 21% by volume of air. It is **very reactive** producing **oxides** with many substances (see page 24). Oxygen is required for two very important reactions: **respiration** and **combustion**.

The essential process of respiration in living organisms requires oxygen.

glucose + oxygen $\rightarrow$ carbon dioxide + water + energy

$C_6H_{12}O_6(s) + 6O_2(g) \rightarrow 6CO_2(g) + 6H_2O + energy$

Combustion of fuels provides us with energy, usually in the form of heat, e.g. methane + oxygen $\rightarrow$ carbon dioxide + water + energy

$CH_4(g) + O_2(g) \rightarrow CO_2(g) + H_2O(g) + energy$

Oxygen is used in the manufacture of sulphuric acid (Contact process) and the manufacture of steel. In hospitals it is used to help patients breathe and is carried by deep sea divers, astronauts and aeroplanes.

Test for oxygen: relights a glowing splint.

Periodic table

1	2											3	4	5	6	7	0
		H															He
Li	Be											B	C	N	O	F	Ne
Na	Mg				transition metals							Al	Si	P	S	Cl	Ar
K	Ca	Sc	Ti	V	Cr	Mn	Fe	Co	Ni	Cu	Zn	Ga	Ge	As	Se	Br	Kr
Rb	Sr	Y	Zr	Nb	Mo	Tc	Ru	Rh	Pd	Ag	Cd	In	Sn	Sb	Te	I	Xe
Cs	Ba	La	Hf	Ta	W	Re	Os	Ir	Pt	Au	Hg	Tl	Pd	Bi	Po	At	Rn

reactive metals   less reactive metals   non-metals

The Periodic Table classifies the elements.
- The elements are listed in order of increasing atomic number.
- Elements with **similar properties** are placed in vertical **Groups**. Elements within a Group have the **same number** of electrons in the **outer shell**.
- There are **8** main groups plus a block of **transition metals**.
- The **more reactive metals** are on the **left-hand side** of the Table.
- The **less reactive metals** are in the **middle block**.
- The **non-metals** are on the **right-hand side** of the Table.
- There is a gradual **change** in **reactivity** and **properties** from the **top** of a Group to the **bottom**.
- **Metals** are **more reactive** at the **bottom** of the Group.
- **Non-metals** are **more reactive** at the **top** of the Group.
- Group 8(0) (the noble gases) is chemically unreactive – full outer shell of electrons.

pH

pH measures the **acidity** of a solution. The pH of any solution can be found using universal indicator. It can be used as a solution or as universal indicator paper which has different colours for each pH value from pH1, strong acid to pH 14 strong alkali!

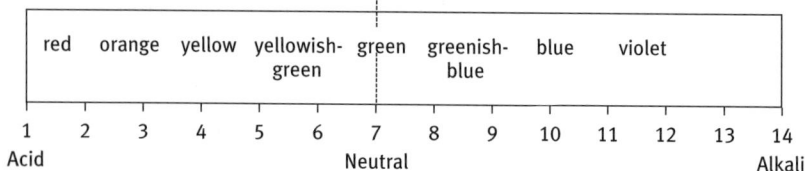

red	orange	yellow	yellowish-green	green	greenish-blue	blue	violet

1	2	3	4	5	6	7	8	9	10	11	12	13	14
Acid						Neutral							Alkali

See also   Indicators and the pH scale

Pollution, air

Pollutant	Source	Harmful effect	Possible solution
Carbon monoxide	Vehicle engines due to incomplete combustion of hydrocarbons.	At low levels – headaches and dizziness. Levels of 1% will kill.	Catalytic converters (to CO_2).
Sulphur dioxide	Combustion of fuels in power stations and extraction of metals from their ores.	Acid rain; bronchitis, asthma and lung disease.	Spray calcium oxide (quicklime) into lakes. Calcium oxide neutralises combustion gases before leaving the chimneys of power stations.
Nitrogen oxides (NO_x)	High temperatures in vehicle engines.	Acid rain; irritate breathing passages.	Catalytic converters (to N_2).
Hydro-carbons	Vehicles, fuel burning in factories, decaying plant material.	Photochemical smog and the greenhouse effect.	Catalytic converters (to CO_2, H_2O).
Soot and smoke	Combustion of fuels including coal-burning power stations.	Smog.	Filters, sprays of water, electrostatic precipitators.
Lead	Petrol in vehicle engines.	Low levels – depression, headaches, tiredness. High levels – brain, liver and kidney damage.	Unleaded petrol. LRP – lead replacement petrol.

Polymers are long chain giant molecules formed during the process of polymerisation in which many small molecules (monomers) are joined together. For example, ethene polymerises to form the polymer poly(ethene) (polythene).

ethene molecules (monomers)

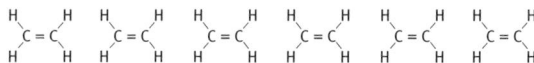

$$\overset{H}{\underset{H}{C}}=\overset{H}{\underset{H}{C}} \quad \overset{H}{\underset{H}{C}}=\overset{H}{\underset{H}{C}} \quad \overset{H}{\underset{H}{C}}=\overset{H}{\underset{H}{C}} \quad \overset{H}{\underset{H}{C}}=\overset{H}{\underset{H}{C}} \quad \overset{H}{\underset{H}{C}}=\overset{H}{\underset{H}{C}} \quad \overset{H}{\underset{H}{C}}=\overset{H}{\underset{H}{C}}$$

↓ polymerisation

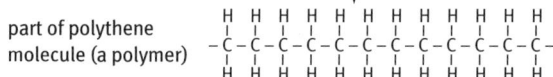

part of polythene molecule (a polymer)

$$-\underset{H}{\overset{H}{C}}-\underset{H}{\overset{H}{C}}-\underset{H}{\overset{H}{C}}-\underset{H}{\overset{H}{C}}-\underset{H}{\overset{H}{C}}-\underset{H}{\overset{H}{C}}-\underset{H}{\overset{H}{C}}-\underset{H}{\overset{H}{C}}-\underset{H}{\overset{H}{C}}-\underset{H}{\overset{H}{C}}-\underset{H}{\overset{H}{C}}-\underset{H}{\overset{H}{C}}-$$

- Polythene is a solid.
- It is unreactive since it contains single bonds.
- Used for making plastic bags, buckets, bowls, etc.

This is an example of **addition polymerisation**. The monomers are able to add onto each other because they have a **double bond** ($C = C$).

Rates of reactions

The **rates** of chemical reactions affect our everyday lives. For example, we need to know how long it takes to boil an egg, to bake a cake, for milk to turn sour, etc. In a chemical reaction the starting materials are called **reactants** and the materials formed are called **products**. The time taken for reactants to form products (rates of reaction) vary enormously. The **rusting of iron** has a very **slow** reaction rate, whereas the reaction of **hydrogen with oxygen** to produce water vapour (**an explosion**) has an extremely **fast** reaction rate.

It is sometimes necessary to be able to change the rate of a chemical reaction. There are four important factors which affect the rate of chemical reactions:

- catalysts (see page 29)
- concentration (see page 29)
- surface area (see page 29)
- temperature (see page 30)

Rates of reactions – calculations

The rate of a chemical reaction is often measured:

- **by the amount of reactant used per unit of time** or
- **by the amount of product produced per unit of time.**

For example, the reaction between calcium carbonate and hydrochloric acid:

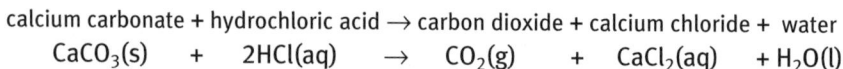

calcium carbonate + hydrochloric acid → carbon dioxide + calcium chloride + water

$$CaCO_3(s) \quad + \quad 2HCl(aq) \quad \rightarrow \quad CO_2(g) \quad + \quad CaCl_2(aq) \quad + H_2O(l)$$

The **rate of the reaction** can be found by measuring the **decrease** in **mass** during the reaction as **carbon dioxide** is given off.

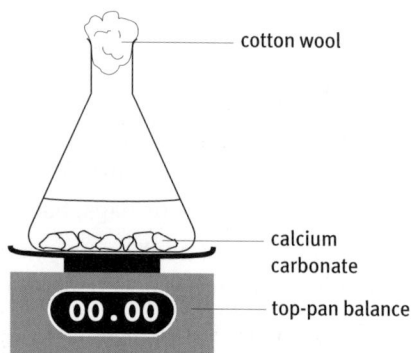

cotton wool

calcium carbonate

00.00

top-pan balance

The mass of the flask and its contents is measured at various times and the rate of the reaction found by plotting mass loss against time.

The **amount** of **product** ($CO_2(g)$) formed can be measured by its increase in volume using a syringe.

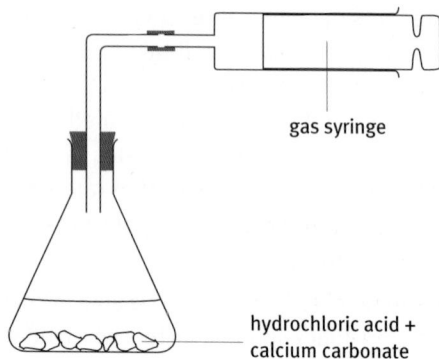

gas syringe

hydrochloric acid + calcium carbonate

The volume of gas in the syringe is noted at various times and the rate of the reaction found by plotting a graph of volume against time.

Rates of reactions – catalysts

A catalyst is a substance that speeds up the rate of a reaction but remains chemically unchanged itself.

Catalysts are very important in industry as they allow manufacturers to produce their products more rapidly, e.g. Contact process (H_2SO_4) and the Haber process (NH_3).

Enzymes are biological catalysts, i.e. they speed up chemical reactions that occur in living things. Enzymes in yeast catalyse the conversion of ethanol to carbon dioxide (fermentation). Enzymes in bacteria convert milk to yoghurt and cheese.

Rates of reactions – concentration effect

The rate of a reaction is increased when the concentration of the reactants is increased.

Rates of reactions – surface area effect

Generally reaction rates are increased when the surface area is increased. The reaction between marble chips (calcium carbonate) and dilute hydrochloric acid can be used to show how changing the surface area of a substance can alter the rate of a reaction.

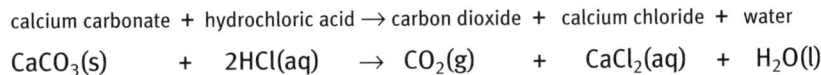

calcium carbonate + hydrochloric acid → carbon dioxide + calcium chloride + water

$$CaCO_3(s) \quad + \quad 2HCl(aq) \quad \rightarrow \quad CO_2(g) \quad + \quad CaCl_2(aq) \quad + \quad H_2O(l)$$

The rate of the reaction can be found by measuring the decrease in mass (see page 28).

Increasing the surface area allows more of the marble to be in contact with the acid.

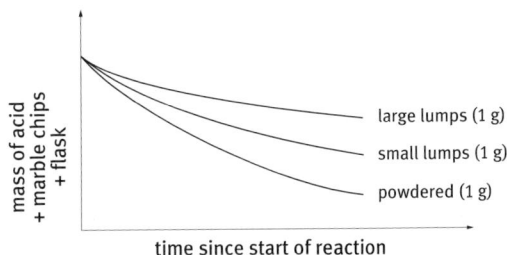

large lumps (1 g)
small lumps (1 g)
powdered (1 g)

mass of acid + marble chips + flask

time since start of reaction

Rates of reactions – temperature effect

Chemical reactions can be made to go faster or slower by changing the temperature of the reactants.

Reducing the temperature lowers the rate of reaction.

Raising the temperature increases the rate of the reaction.

The reaction between **sodium thiosulphate** solution and dilute **hydrochloric acid** can be used to study the effect of temperature on the rate of a reaction.

The solution goes cloudy due to the formation of solid sulphur.

The time taken for the pencil cross to disappear is measured at different temperatures. As the temperature is increased the cross disappears more quickly. The rate of the reaction increases.

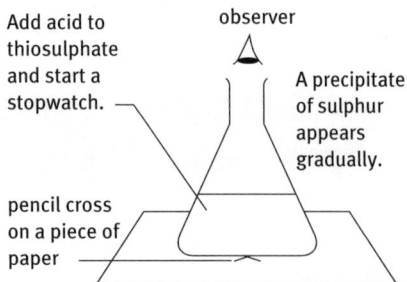

Add acid to thiosulphate and start a stopwatch.

observer

A precipitate of sulphur appears gradually.

pencil cross on a piece of paper

Reacting masses

The equation of a chemical reaction enables us to calculate the amount of substance used and the amount of substance produced.

Examples

1 Calculate the mass of magnesium oxide produced from the complete oxidation of 48 g of magnesium (A_r Mg = 24, O = 16) (see page 31).

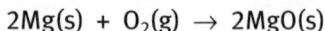

$$2Mg(s) + O_2(g) \rightarrow 2MgO(s)$$

A_r Mg = 24, M_r MgO = 40 (see page 37 for M_r)

2 moles of magnesium produces 2 moles of magnesium oxide.

∴ 48 g of magnesium produces 80 g of magnesium oxide.

2 Calculate the mass of copper oxide formed from the breakdown of 62 g of copper carbonate.

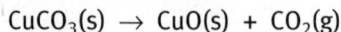

$$CuCO_3(s) \rightarrow CuO(s) + CO_2(g)$$

(A_r Cu = 64, C = 12, O = 16)

$M_r CuCO_3 = 64 + 12 + (3 \times 16) = 124$, $M_r CuO = 64 + 16 = 80$

124 g $CuCO_3$ forms 80 g CuO

∴ 62 g $CuCO_3$ forms 40 g CuO

Reactivity series of metals

The reactivity series lists metals in order of their reactivity.

The table below shows the reactivity of metals with oxygen, water and acid.

	Water	Acid	Oxygen	
Potassium	react violently	react	burn easily,	most
Sodium	with	violently	bright	reactive
Calcium	cold water		flame	
Magnesium				
Aluminium	react when	react		
(Carbon)	heated	quite		
Zinc	in steam	fast	react more	
Iron			slowly when	
Tin		slow	heated	
Lead		reaction		
(Hydrogen)				
Copper	no reaction	no		
Silver		reaction		
Gold		(below	no	least
Platinum		hydrogen)	reaction	reactive

Relative atomic mass

The **relative atomic mass** of an atom is the number of **protons** and **neutrons** present in the nucleus, added together. Relative atomic mass has the symbol A_r. The **atomic number** is the number of **protons** in the **nucleus**. The **Periodic Table** arranges elements in order of increasing atomic number. It also gives their relative atomic masses.

$$40 \longleftarrow \text{relative atomic mass}$$

E.g. $\quad \text{Ca}$

$$20 \longleftarrow \text{atomic number}$$

Calcium has 20 protons (atomic number = 20) and 20 neutrons:

relative atomic mass – atomic number = $40 - 20 = 20n$.

Some atoms have masses which are not whole numbers, e.g. chlorine has a mass of 35.5. This is because it is possible for an element to have atoms with different numbers of neutrons and so different atomic masses, called **isotopes**. The A_r is the average of the isotopic masses, e.g. Cl = 35.5, weighted average of ^{35}Cl and ^{37}Cl.

Rusting of iron and steel

Air, **water** and **acid** attack metals causing them to **corrode**. Corrosion to **iron** and **steel** is called **rusting**. For rusting to occur both air and water must be present.

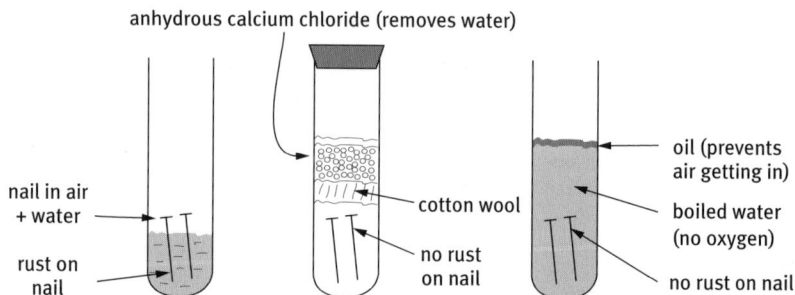

anhydrous calcium chloride (removes water)

nail in air + water

rust on nail

cotton wool

no rust on nail

oil (prevents air getting in)

boiled water (no oxygen)

no rust on nail

- Iron and steel are **weakened** by rusting and are **expensive** to repair.
- Methods used to try to **protect** these metals from rusting generally involve **coating** the metal to keep out the air and water, e.g. painting, grease/oil, plastic, chrome plating.
- **Sacrificial protection** involves attaching lumps of a more reactive metal to the metal which needs protection, e.g. magnesium on underwater pipes.

Salts

Many salts occur **naturally** in the Earth's crust. The most common and useful of these is **sodium chloride (common salt)**.

- Used in the **food industry**.
- **Electrolysis** produces sodium hydroxide, chlorine, hydrogen.
- **Rock salt** contains grit and salt – spread on icy roads in winter.
- Used to manufacture other useful salts, such as sodium carbonate (washing soda) and sodium hydrogen carbonate (baking soda).

Salts are used in a wide variety of ways including:

- photographic film – silver bromide
- toothpastes – calcium fluoride
- fungicide – copper(II) sulphate
- fertilisers – ammonium nitrate, ammonium sulphate.

Salts – making insoluble salts

To make an **insoluble salt, two solutions** are mixed together to form a **precipitate**. The precipitate is then **separated** from the rest of the mixture by **filtration** or **centrifugation**.

Example

barium chloride + sodium sulphate $\rightarrow$ barium sulphate + sodium chloride

$$BaCl_2(aq) \quad + \quad Na_2SO_4(aq) \quad \rightarrow \quad BaSO_4(s) \quad + \quad 2NaCl(aq)$$

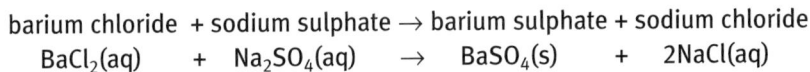

This can be written as the ionic equation:

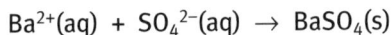

$$Ba^{2+}(aq) + SO_4{}^{2-}(aq) \rightarrow BaSO_4(s)$$

Exam tip

To precipitate an insoluble salt a solution containing its positive metal ions must be mixed with a solution containing its negative non-metal ions.

Salts – making soluble salts

There are **four methods** for making a soluble salt. All involve the **neutralisation** of an **acid**.

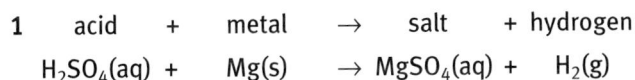

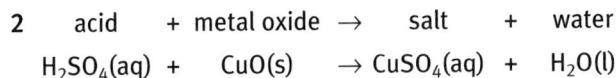

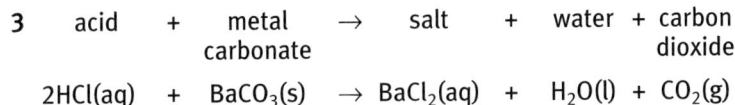

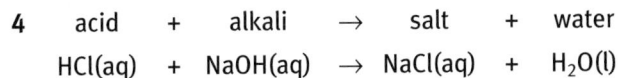

1   acid   +   metal $\rightarrow$ salt   + hydrogen

    $H_2SO_4(aq)$ + $Mg(s)$ $\rightarrow MgSO_4(aq)$ + $H_2(g)$

2   acid   + metal oxide $\rightarrow$ salt   +   water

    $H_2SO_4(aq)$ + $CuO(s)$ $\rightarrow CuSO_4(aq)$ + $H_2O(l)$

3   acid   +   metal $\rightarrow$ salt   +   water + carbon
                    carbonate   dioxide

    $2HCl(aq)$ + $BaCO_3(s)$ $\rightarrow BaCl_2(aq)$ + $H_2O(l)$ + $CO_2(g)$

4   acid   +   alkali $\rightarrow$ salt   +   water

    $HCl(aq)$ + $NaOH(aq)$ $\rightarrow NaCl(aq)$ + $H_2O(l)$

(see **Titrations** page 37)

Saturated solutions

A saturated solution is a solution that contains as much dissolved solute as possible at a given temperature. No more solute is able to dissolve at that temperature.

If the saturated solution is heated more sugar is able to dissolve.

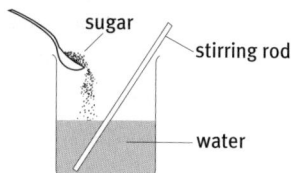

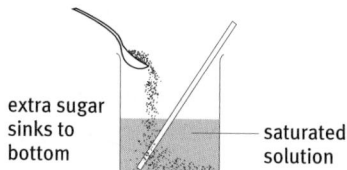

sugar
stirring rod
water

extra sugar sinks to bottom
saturated solution

Solubility

Solubility is the number of grams of a substance that will dissolve in 100 grams of water (solvent) at a given temperature.

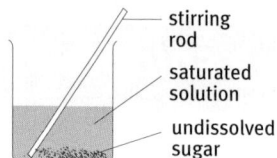

stirring rod
saturated solution
undissolved sugar

now there is less sugar at the bottom

all the sugar has dissolved

At 20°C
This solution is saturated – undissolved crystals at the bottom of the beaker.

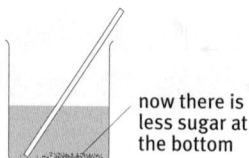

At 50°C
More sugar has dissolved, but the solution is still saturated.

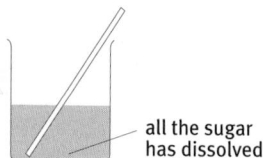

At 80°C
The solution is just saturated.

Example

21 grams of magnesium chloride dissolve in 70 grams of water at 50°C. What is the solubility of magnesium chloride in water at 50°C?

Solubility = mass dissolved in 100 g of water.

1 gram of water will dissolve $= \dfrac{21}{70}$ g of magnesium chloride

therefore

100 grams of water will dissolve $\dfrac{21}{70}$ x 100 $= 30$ g of magnesium chloride

Solubility of magnesium chloride in water **at 50°C is 30 g/100 g water.**

Solvents

A solvent is a liquid able to dissolve another substance. **Water** is the most important solvent. The solutions formed when water is the solvent are called **aqueous solutions**. Many other solvents are also very important to us in our everyday lives. These solvents are used to dissolve substances that are **insoluble** (will not dissolve) in water. They are generally called **organic solvents**. Examples are:

- **ethanol** – used as a solvent in paints, varnishes and perfumes
- **propanone** – dissolves grease and nail polish
- **trichloroethane** – dissolves the white pigment in liquid paper.

Organic solvents evaporate quickly at room temperature, so paints, glue, etc. dry quickly.

States of matter

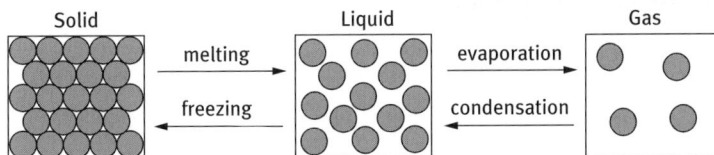

Solid   melting / freezing → Liquid   evaporation / condensation → Gas

Solids	Liquids	Gases
have a fixed shape and volume. They are made up of particles packed closely together. The particles vibrate but cannot move around due to the strong forces of attraction between them.	have a definite volume but no fixed shape – they take the shape of their container. The particles are close together but are free to move around. The forces holding them together are weaker than in solids.	fill whatever container they are placed in. The particles move freely and are far apart as there are only very weak forces of attraction between them.

Changes of state

When a solid is heated it changes to a liquid. The particles get more energy, vibrate more and overcome the forces of attraction that hold them in the solid state. Similarly when a liquid is heated it changes to a gas (evaporates). Each liquid has a boiling point – the temperature at which it boils and turns to a gas. The opposite occurs on cooling, i.e. gases condense to form liquids; liquids freeze forming solids.

Sulphuric acid

Manufactured using the **Contact process.** Starting materials are **sulphur, air** and **water.**

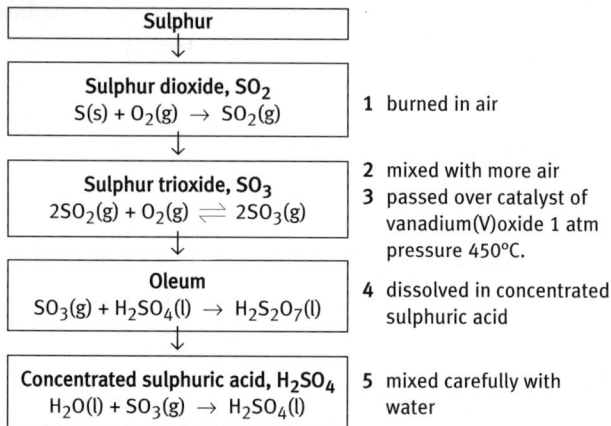

Sulphur
↓

Sulphur dioxide, SO_2
$S(s) + O_2(g) \rightarrow SO_2(g)$

1 burned in air

↓

Sulphur trioxide, SO_3
$2SO_2(g) + O_2(g) \rightleftharpoons 2SO_3(g)$

2 mixed with more air
3 passed over catalyst of vanadium(V)oxide 1 atm pressure 450°C.

↓

Oleum
$SO_3(g) + H_2SO_4(l) \rightarrow H_2S_2O_7(l)$

4 dissolved in concentrated sulphuric acid

↓

Concentrated sulphuric acid, H_2SO_4
$H_2O(l) + SO_3(g) \rightarrow H_2SO_4(l)$

5 mixed carefully with water

Used to make fertilisers, detergents, plastics and for battery acid.

Thermosetting and thermosoftening plastics

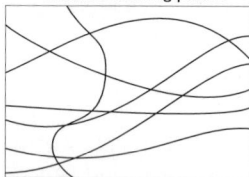

Plastics can be divided into two groups according to the way in which they behave on heating. This is due to differences in their structures.

Thermosoftening plastic

Thermosetting plastic

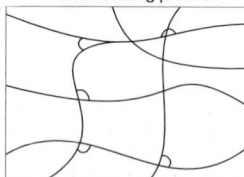

- **Thermosoftening plastics** are made up of many long polymer chains. The **attraction** between the chains is very **weak**. When heated the weak attractions are overcome and the plastic melts. On cooling the forces of attraction return and the plastic solidifies. This process of heating and cooling can be repeated many times.

- **Thermosetting plastics** contain many long polymer chains which interact with each other, forming **cross-linkages**. A huge 3-dimensional structure is formed. These plastics are **resistant** to **heat**.

They are extremely useful but can be environmentally unfriendly. They may produce toxic fumes when burnt and so be hard to dispose of if they are non-biodegradable.

Method used to measure the concentration of a solution.

1 A measured volume of alkali is placed in a conical flask. A few drops of indicator are added. The flask sits on a white tile.

2 The volume of acid in the burette is recorded.

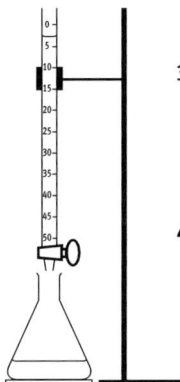

3 Acid is added slowly to the alkali, whilst the conical flask is swirled gently. When the indicator changes to its neutral colour, no more acid is added.

4 The volume of acid in the burette is recorded. The volume of acid used is calculated.

Calculations

20 cm^3 of hydrochloric acid neutralised 25 cm^3 of a 0.25 mol/dm^3 sodium hydroxide solution. What was the concentration of the hydrochloric acid?

- Write a balanced equation for the reaction.
    $HCl(aq) + NaOH(aq) \rightarrow NaCl(aq) + H_2O(l)$
    1 mol of HCl neutralises 1 mol of NaOH.
- You know the concentration of the NaOH, and can therefore work out the number of moles of NaOH.
    No. of moles of NaOH = volume (dm^3) x concentration (mol/dm^3)
    $= 0.025 \times 0.25 = 0.00625$ mol
- You can now work out the concentration of HCl:
    You know that 1 mol of NaOH reacts with 1 mol of HCl
    therefore 0.00625 mol of NaOH reacts with 0.00625 mol of HCl
    No. of moles of HCl = volume of HCl x concentration of HCl
    (dm^3)   (mol/dm^3)
    0.00625 mol = 0.02 x concentration of HCl
    concentration of HCl = $\dfrac{0.00625}{0.020 \text{ dm}^3}$mol = 0.3125 mol/dm^3

Transition metals

They lie between Groups 2 and 3 in the Periodic Table. Examples are copper, iron, cobalt, nickel and chromium. They:

- form coloured compounds
- form ions with variable charge, e.g. Fe^{2+}, Fe^{3+}
- have high m.pt/b.pt, high densities.
- act as catalysts

Water cycle

5 Clouds are blown by the wind. As they rise over higher ground, larger drops of water form.

4 Water vapour cools and condenses to form clouds of tiny droplets.

3 Transpiration in plants produces water vapour.

6 Water returns to land and sea as rain and snow.

2 Respiration in plants and animals produces water vapour.

1 Warmed by the sun, water evaporates from oceans, rivers and lakes.

7 Rain collects in streams.

8 Streams flow into rivers. Rivers flow into the sea, completing the cycle.

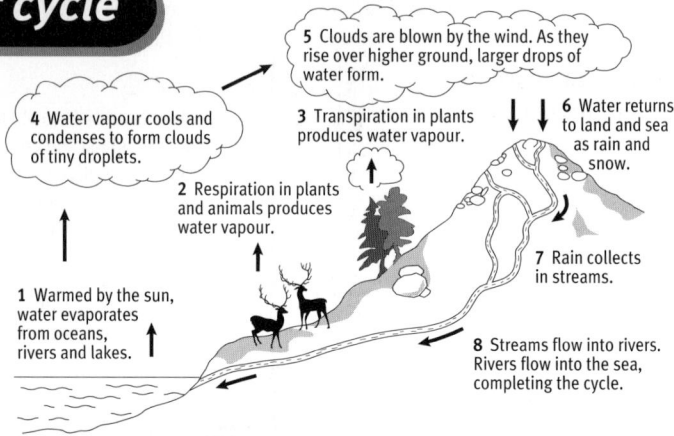

Water pollution

Harmful substances from a variety of sources are constantly finding their way into our **coastal waters, rivers, lakes and estuaries**, i.e. our water is being **polluted**. Some of the sources of pollution are listed below.

- **Industry** – waste liquids from factories contain substances such as **mercury** and **lead** which are highly poisonous. **Radioactive waste** from nuclear power stations and nuclear waste processing plants. Burning coal and oil in power stations releases sulphur dioxide and oxides of nitrogen into the atmosphere, producing **acid rain**. This poisons rivers and lakes killing fish and other aquatic life.
- **Fertilisers** – excess can be washed out of the soil by rainwater and into the groundwater used for drinking. Thought that **nitrates** from the fertilisers may cause cancers. Fertilisers drain into rivers and lakes aiding the growth of algae, which eventually covers the surface of the water, blocking out light. The plants below are unable grow. They die and decay using up dissolved oxygen. Fish become starved of oxygen and die. The lake is no longer able to support life. This process is called **eutrophication**.
- **Sewage** – released into rivers untreated, contains bacteria causing disease to humans. Bacteria also use up the dissolved oxygen.
- **Heat** – industries use river water as a coolant which is then returned to the river at high temperatures. Oxygen is less soluble at high temperatures, therefore causes a problem for aquatic life.
- **Oil** – accidents involving oil tankers result in oil spillages into the sea which poison fish, kill sea birds (glues their feathers).